Polar Bear Family
Adventures

Bobbie Kalman

Crabtree Publishing Company

www.crabtreebooks.com

Animal Family ADVENTURES

Created by Bobbie Kalman

For Timothée Duquesne,
with love from Bobbie, Peter, and Samantha.
We can't wait to have fun with you
in Niagara Falls!

Author
Bobbie Kalman

Editors
Kathy Middleton
Crystal Sikkens

Photo research
Bobbie Kalman

Design
Bobbie Kalman
Katherine Berti

Print and production coordinator
Katherine Berti

Illustrations
Barb Hinterhoeller: page 27

Photographs
© Sabin, Robert / Animals Animals: pages 13 (bottom),
   14, 15
Dreamstime: page 16 (bottom)
iStockphoto: page 22
Mitsuaki Iwago/Minden Pictures: page 6
Superstock: Steve Bloom Images: page 10; Juniors:
   pages 13 (top), 20–21
Thinkstock: pages 24–25, 30 (bottom left)
U.S. Fish and Wildlife Service/Wikimedia Commons:
   page 12 (top)
Cover and all other images by Shutterstock

Library and Archives Canada Cataloguing in Publication

Kalman, Bobbie, author
   Polar bear family adventures / Bobbie Kalman.

(Animal family adventures)
Includes index.
Issued in print and electronic formats.
ISBN 978-0-7787-2228-1 (bound).--ISBN 978-0-7787-2236-6
(paperback).--ISBN 978-1-4271-1712-0 (html)

      1. Polar bear--Juvenile literature. 2. Polar bear--Infancy--
Juvenile literature. I. Title.

QL737.C27K3477 2016   j599.786   C2015-908690-6
                                               C2015-908691-4

Library of Congress Cataloging-in-Publication Data

CIP available at Library of Congress

Crabtree Publishing Company
www.crabtreebooks.com   1-800-387-7650

Printed in Canada/052016/TL20160324

Published in Canada
Crabtree Publishing
616 Welland Ave.
St. Catharines, Ontario
L2M 5V6

Published in the United States
Crabtree Publishing
PMB 59051
350 Fifth Avenue, 59th Floor
New York, New York 10118

Published in the United Kingdom
Crabtree Publishing
Maritime House
Basin Road North, Hove
BN41 1WR

Published in Australia
Crabtree Publishing
3 Charles Street
Coburg North
VIC 3058

What is in this book?

Meet the polar bears!

Polar bears live in the **Arctic**, an icy cold place in the most northern part of Earth. In October, a mother polar bear digs a **den** deep in the snow on the side of a hill. Inside the den, the snow protects her and keeps her warm. In December, two tiny **cubs**, or babies, are born in the den.

Polar bears are **mammals**. Like all mammals, they have hair or fur on their bodies, and they are born live.

Mother mammals **nurse**, or feed their babies milk from their bodies. The cubs, whom we shall call Sesi and Tika, spend most of their time cuddled up to their mother, Nanuk. They nurse often because their stomachs can only hold about a spoonful of milk at a time. As they grow, the cubs will nurse less often. Nanuk will teach them how to swim, hunt, and survive in the Arctic. After about two-and-a-half-years, the cubs will leave Nanuk to live on their own.

Warm and fuzzy

When spring arrives and the sun starts to shine again in the Arctic, Sesi and Tika climb out of their den for the first time. It is colder outside the den, and the wind is blowing, but the cubs do not feel cold. Their bodies are covered with a layer of **blubber**, or fat, and two kinds of fur. Next to their skin, there is an undercoat of short fur, which keeps them warm. An outer layer of guard hairs keeps water away from their skin.

Sesi and Tika's fur looks white, but their hairs are actually hollow and clear. Their skin underneath is black. You can see the black skin on Sesi's nose, mouth, and chin. His black skin also shows through his fur.

Like all bears, Tika walks on all four legs, but she can also walk on just her back legs. She holds out her large padded paws to help keep her balance. Polar bears have five toes with claws on each foot. They also have fur between their toes, as well as small bumps on the bottom of their paws. The claws and bumps grip the ice and snow and help keep the bears from slipping.

Learning to walk

Nanuk and her cubs must soon start a long walk from land to the **sea ice,** where Nanuk will find seals to hunt. Seals are the main food of polar bears. Nanuk has not eaten for more than seven months! She has been living off the fat stored on her body, but she must eat soon. Her body needs more fat so it can keep making milk for her cubs. Sesi and Tika must keep up with Nanuk on their journey, so they practice walking near the den.

Sesi finds it hard to climb out of the den with his mother. He has to climb up over the snow.

Tika has made it out and is walking carefully. Oops, she fell. She may need to practice walking a bit more, but for now, she enjoys rolling in the snow. It's fun!

The world outside

After months of being in a dark den, the world outside looks exciting to the cubs! Nanuk keeps them close to the den for at least two weeks. Sesi and Tika need time to get used to the huge outdoors, and they need to be strong enough to walk a long way. If there is any sign of danger or bad weather, Sesi and Tika can quickly go back into their den, where they are safe.

Outside the den, Nanuk rolls around in the snow to clean her fur, and Sesi and Tika play in the snow.

As Nanuk nurses Sesi, she wonders where Tika went. Tika is having fun exploring her new white world!

Fun with Mom

Sesi and Tika love to snuggle and play with their mother. They climb on her back and lick and kiss her.

Sesi wants to have a game of tag, but after playing with her cubs, Nanuk needs a rest. Sesi chases Tika across the snow but seems to be losing the race. He is not happy about that at all. "Hey! Not so fast, Tika! I want to win."

Time to leave home

A few days later, Nanuk feels Tika and Sesi are ready to make the long journey from their den out to the sea ice. Sea ice is frozen water that forms in the ocean. It grows in the winter and melts in the summer, but there is usually some sea ice all year long. It is where Nanuk can find ringed seals, the main kind of seals that she hunts. Sesi and Tika have a lot to learn about hunting, but Nanuk will teach them everything they need to know to survive in their icy home.

Nanuk and Sesi spot a male polar bear in the distance. Male polar bears sometimes eat cubs when they are very hungry. Nanuk has to make sure he does not see her babies.

Sesi and Tika start walking beside Nanuk.

Nanuk's large body hides the cubs.

Arctic land animals

As Nanuk and her cubs walk across the land to the ocean, they see other animals that live in the Arctic. Sesi spots something far away. Is it one of the animals shown on the next page?

Arctic fox

Arctic wolf

Does Sesi see an Arctic fox, Arctic wolf, Arctic hare, or a white weasel? All these animals live on the Arctic land. In winter, they have thick white fur to keep them warm. Their white fur also makes them hard to spot in the snow.

Arctic hare

white weasel

Finding seals to hunt

Nanuk and her cubs finally reach the sea ice. Like all polar bears, Nanuk is a **carnivore**. Carnivores eat other animals. Nanuk eats mainly ringed seals because there are many of them.

Seals are mammals. They must come up out of the water to breathe air. They cut breathing holes in the ice using their sharp claws. Polar bears can smell seals even if they are far away or under the ice. They wait by the breathing holes for the seals to come up for air.

Ringed seal pups are born in snow dens on top of the ice. Their mother nurses them for about two months. Polar bears find the pups easy to hunt because they cannot swim away. They **pounce**, or jump, on the pups while they lie on the ice. About half the seals that Nanuk hunts are newborn pups. Nanuk needs to gain a lot of fat, so she eats any seal that she can easily hunt.

Sea-ice dining tables

For most of the year, sea ice is covered with snow, but in spring, the snow and ice start to melt. Sea ice is very important to polar bears. They use the ice like a table and drag the seals they hunt onto it. Ice is important to seals, too. Seals live in the ocean under the ice and give birth to their pups on top of it. There would be fewer seals without sea ice.

Nanuk has hunted a seal and is dragging it onto the ice so she and her cubs can eat it. Tika and Sesi smell the seal's blood in the snow and look forward to eating their meal. Even though they are still nursing, they will now also eat seal meat.

Learning from Mom

Sesi and Tika learn how to hunt seals from their mother. They must stay very still while Nanuk hunts so they do not scare away a seal before she can grab it. Sesi and Tika also learn to clean themselves after they eat. They rub their heads in the snow and roll around in it to clean their fur.

Summer has begun, and the sea ice is melting quickly. Nanuk teaches her cubs how to jump from one piece of ice to another. The cubs also learn to swim so they can travel in the ocean when the ice has melted. Polar bears are excellent swimmers!

Look and find

Polar bears are born on land but, as adults, they spend most of their time in the ocean. That is why they are called **marine**, or ocean, mammals. Seals, walruses, and whales are other marine mammals. Birds are not mammals. Which other animal in this picture is not a mammal?

Arctic terns

beluga whales

polar bear

walruses

long-tailed
duck

narwhal

Arctic
cod

This picture shows six kinds of birds that visit or live in the Arctic. Do some research on one or more of these birds.

puffins

Arctic skuas

guillemots

spotted seals

polar bears

harp seals

sea gulls

bearded seal

Answer
Arctic cod are fish.
Fish are not mammals.

ribbon seal

ringed seal

Winter is coming!

Autumn has arrived, and the cubs have put on a lot of weight by eating the seals they helped their mother hunt. They will now go back to land and help their mother dig a bigger den than the one in which they were born. Sesi and Tika have learned a lot from Nanuk, but their mother will still need to feed and protect them for another year or two. Winter will soon be here, and there will not be any sunlight until the spring. Polar bear mothers and their cubs spend this freezing cold time under the snow. Male polar bears and females without cubs do not make dens. They stay active and look for food during winter.

The new den will
have two rooms.

Sesi and Tika can play in
one room while Nanuk
sleeps in the other.

Did you know?

Polar bear cubs learn their fighting and hunting skills by play-fighting with each other. Fighting is also a way to test how strong they are. Adult males also play-fight. When they do, they look like they are dancing! Make up a polar bear dance to do with your friends!

Animals lose body heat through their ears and tails. Polar bears have small round ears and short tails, which help them keep heat inside their bodies. Their claws are thick, curved, and strong. Polar bears use their claws to catch and hold their prey.

Polar bear mothers often carry their cubs on their backs. Sometimes they pick them up by their necks or ears!

The **climate** on Earth is changing. Warmer temperatures are making ocean waters in the Arctic warmer, too. Sea ice is melting faster, leaving less time for seals to have pups and for polar bears to hunt them. Fewer seals mean less food for Nanuk, Sesi, and Tika.

Match them up!

The pictures on these pages will help you remember what you have learned about polar bears. Match the pictures to the information in the box on the next page.

Match the pictures with this information.

1. Sesi and Tika practice their hunting skills by play-fighting.
2. Polar bears hunt and eat seals on sea ice.
3. Polar bear cubs live with their mother for two-and-a-half years.
4. Nanuk uses her sense of smell to find seals under ice.
5. Polar bear cubs are born in dens dug under snow.
6. Polar bear mothers teach their cubs how to swim. What else do the mothers teach their cubs?

Answers

1. A, 2. C, 3. F, 4. B, 5. D, 6. E, C. (hunting)

Words to know

Note: Some boldfaced words are defined where they appear in the book.

Arctic (AHRK-tik) noun Relating to the cold, icy area near the North Pole

blubber (BLUHB-er) noun A thick layer of fat under an animal's skin

carnivore (KAHR-nuh-vawr) noun An animal that hunts and eats other animals

climate (KLAHY-mit) noun The normal, long-term weather conditions in an area

den (den) noun A shelter used to have babies or for a long winter sleep

mammal (MAM-uh-l) noun A warm-blooded animal that is covered in hair or fur and gives birth to live young

marine (muh-REEN) adjective Describing an animal that lives in the ocean

pounce (pouns) verb To spring or leap suddenly to catch prey

prey (prey) noun An animal that is hunted and eaten by another animal

sea ice (see ahys) noun Frozen water that forms, grows, and melts in the ocean

A noun is a person, place, or thing. A verb is an action word that tells you what someone or something does. An adjective is a word that tells you what something is like.

Index